Contents

We eat to live

All living creatures need food to live. Your body turns food into energy for your muscles and brain. Food also helps you to grow – and eating it is enjoyable too!

Machines need fuel to keep working. A car has to be filled with petrol or it will stop moving. Our bodies need fuel too.

Sometimes your stomach grumbles when you're hungry, or your throat feels dry and you need to drink. Your body is telling you what it wants. Feeling hungry and thirsty are called reflexes – you do them without thinking.

Eating will make you strong. The food you eat acts like hundreds of little workers. They develop your muscles, brighten up your brain and strengthen your organs. They help your lungs to breathe and your heart to pump blood through your veins. They can also repair some of your body's problems and help it fight diseases.

When you eat, you grow. A newborn baby weighs just a few kilograms, and is about 50 centimetres long. A few months later, it has grown heavier and taller. Milk and baby food have worked their magic!

Eating is fun! Eating isn't just something you do to survive. It's also enjoyable, and often at the centre of a celebration. There's nothing like sharing a meal of mouth-watering food with friends or family. Eating certain foods can bring back memories. A rice pudding may remind you of winter evenings at Granny's house, and spaghetti might make you think of Sunday meals at home.

Experiment

Plant a tiny seedling in some soil or put some beans on damp cotton wool. To grow a plant you need to give it light, water and good soil.

Food's journey

Food travels through your body – into your mouth, down to your stomach and through your intestines. Along the way, the food is changed in different ways so that your organs, nerves, muscles and brain can take from it what they need.

Imagine you're hungry, so you bite into a peach. You chew, then you swallow ... and a few minutes later you feel better.

Here's what happens inside your body:

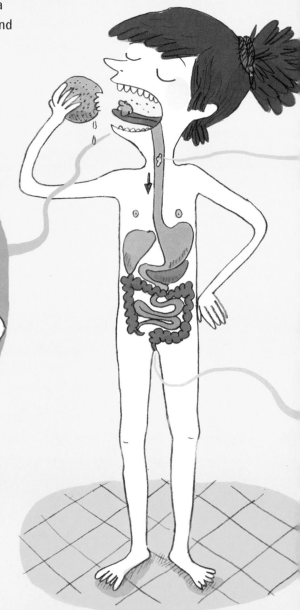

1. Your teeth break the peach into small pieces, and your tongue churns these pieces about like a washing machine.

2. Your saliva works by softening the bits of fruit. This liquid can now be swallowed and is sent down a tube called the oesophagus to your stomach.

OW-OW-OW!

3. The peach is digested in the stomach. It's mixed with gastric juices that change it into microscopic nutrients. These nutrients can now pass through the walls of the small intestine and into the blood. They travel through the arteries and veins (like little rivers) to all the parts of the body that need fuel. The leftover waste moves through the large intestine and is pushed out the anus.

If you eat too quickly and swallow your food in big chunks, you can't digest it properly. Your tummy might swell up and feel sore. You must chew your food first, using your teeth to grind it down – then your stomach can do its job.

Did you know?

The liver and the pancreas are important organs that help digest your food. The liver makes bile which breaks down the fats in food. The pancreas helps to change food into tiny particles that can be used by the body.

How much energy is in food?

Food gives the body energy. But how much energy do people need? It depends on how active and how old they are. Eating a balanced diet means eating enough for your own energy needs. Playing sport burns a lot more energy than watching TV!

Running, walking, singing – even breathing – all use up energy. The energy burned by a gardener is two and a half times greater than the energy used by an office worker. A rower uses nearly nine times more energy than a couch potato!

Just as kilograms measure weight, kilojoules (kJ) measure the amount of energy in food. Foods contain different numbers of kilojoules.

100 g of yoghurt   100 g of croissant   100 g of bread

100 g of banana   100 g of meat and carrots   100 g of steak and fries

The amount of food you eat should match the energy your body burns up. If it doesn't, any extra food is saved as fat which makes you put on weight. This is usually bad for your body. But not eating enough can be just as unhealthy.

Did you know?

Fries aren't always unhealthy. Half an hour of skiing burns up 1000 kJ, which is about the same amount of energy as one serving of fries. After 30 minutes of skiing, you could eat some fries to replace the energy you've lost.

Different roles

Now you know that food allows your body to work, repair itself and grow. All foods are made up of simpler parts called nutrients. Nutrients include sugars, fats, vitamins and minerals. Just as on stage where every actor has a special role, each nutrient has its own role in the body.

SUGARS (or CARBOHYDRATES)

What do they do? Sugars are a source of energy for your body, especially when you are active or playing sport.

Where are they found? Not just in sweet foods. Simple/fast sugars (found in sweets) are very quickly digested. Complex/slow sugars (found in bread) are digested more slowly, and provide energy for the body over several hours.

Simple sugars	Complex sugars
White or brown sugar, sweets, fruit cordial.	Bread, potatoes, rice, pasta.

FATS

What do they do? Some fats are healthy. They provide your body with lots of energy. One gram of sugar has 16 kJ of energy, but one gram of fat has 37 kJ. Some fats are essential for healthy skin, nerves, heart and arteries. We must get these from our food, but in small doses.

Where are they found? In oils, butter and cream. There are also 'hidden' fats in meat and fish, cheese and milk.

VITAMINS

What do they do? There are more than ten different vitamins in food. Each of them plays a very important role in helping our bodies to function. Vitamin A is needed for growth and for skin health. Vitamin C helps us fight off many diseases. Vitamin E makes our red blood cells live longer. The list goes on!

Where are they found? Each food contains one or more vitamins. Butter contains vitamins D and E; fresh fruit contains vitamin C; cereals have vitamin B; and some vegetables are rich in vitamin A.

MINERALS

What do they do? Minerals, like calcium, iron, phosphorus and magnesium, are essential in tiny amounts and help build healthy bones and cells. They're also important for our nervous system and muscles. Copper, fluoride, iodine and zinc are needed too, but in even smaller amounts.

Where are they found? All foods contain at least one of these precious minerals. Milk contains calcium; liver and spinach have iron; and shellfish are a source of iodine.

PROTEINS

What do they do? Proteins are like the building blocks of the body. They build muscles and keep them healthy.

Where are they found? There are proteins in meat, fish and eggs, and also in cereals such as bread, rice, corn and pulses (lentils, baked beans, chickpeas).

WATER

What does it do? 65% of your body is water – that's how important it is! One of its jobs is to help our bodies get rid of waste. It is essential to drink between eight and ten glasses of water every day.

Where is it found? All foods contain some water. For example, 100 g of bread contains 34 g of water, and 100 g of fruit has 80 g of water. Tapwater is usually safe to drink. Some bottled spring water has more minerals.

Experiment

Some foods provide more nutrients than others. A litre of milk has the same amount of energy as about 100 g of quiche (1465 kJ), but milk contains 33 g of protein and the quiche has only 12 g.

Compare these two snacks:

100 g chocolate-filled pastry containing:
0.6 g protein and 1700 kJ energy

100 g of bread and 4 squares of chocolate containing:
0.9g protein and 1490 kJ energy

Which snack would you choose? Why?

Did you know?

No single food is complete or perfect by itself. To get all the nutrients needed for good health, we need to eat a wide variety of foods. This is called a balanced diet.

How taste works

When you put food in your mouth, you can taste it. That's how you can tell the difference between chips and chocolate, and why you like some foods more than others. Your other senses play a role too: how a food smells, what it looks like and how it feels.

Every food has its own taste. When you eat, the taste buds all over your tongue go into action. These tiny sensors send you a signal: the taste of the food. All by itself, the taste is limited to only four sensations: sweet, salty, sour and bitter.

Of course, you can taste more than just four flavours. That's because your nose has a role too. The sense of smell is closely linked to the sense of taste. The nose has a much greater range of sensations than the tongue. That's how you can tell cheddar from edam, even though both cheeses feel the same in your mouth.

Bitter

Cocoa powder, coffee beans, marmalade, grapefruit

Sour

Lemon, gherkins, vinegar

Sweet

Sweets, fruit, honey, cake

Salty

Cheese, salami, bacon

When you eat you use many senses. It's not just taste and smell that affect our experience of what we eat. The sense of touch tells you the difference between hot and cold, the smoothness of a hard-boiled egg, or the silky feeling of the yolk when it's soft-boiled.

What you see helps too. Is the fruit you are about to bite into green or ripe? Is that murky liquid really okay to drink?

Even hearing has a role to play. You hear your teeth crunch into a hard apple or a crusty bread roll, and the bubbles fizzing in lemonade.

18

Experiment

If you can, compare the difference between milk straight from a dairy farm and store-bought milk in a carton. Milk on a farm is untreated and will have a richer smell and flavour. Your tongue may even taste the grass and the animals. Milk from a supermarket has been pasteurised, maybe thinned (skimmed), or heat-treated to make it last longer. It will taste different.

Did you know?

The only taste that babies naturally find attractive is sweetness. Studies of very young babies have shown that they are usually disgusted by sour and bitter flavours, but seem happy with sweet.

A matter of taste

Love watermelon? Hate Brussels sprouts? Crazy about cashew nuts? Everyone has their own likes and dislikes. Taste is an unpredictable and personal thing.

Find out from your friends what foods they do and don't like. Maybe Jonathan only likes pasta without cheese; Sophie doesn't like meat, except ham; and Alex loves stewed (not dried) apricots. Most people seem to like chocolate but what about vegetables? Zoe hated parsnip until she ate it mashed together with carrot. Your friends like different things, which just shows that it takes all sorts!

Imagine a baby who is learning something new every day. If his mother doesn't like asparagus, she may have a disgusted look on her face when she feeds him some. The baby may read his mother's body language and think 'be careful, something's wrong with this'. He's probably not going to like asparagus.

It's hard to know why someone likes or dislikes pumpkin or tomatoes. It all depends on what you are used to eating. Your tastebuds have a very long memory!

Tasting new things is part of growing up. Have you ever been proud of yourself for eating something new, like mushrooms or olives?

Experiment

Hold your nose when you bite into a toasted ham and cheese sandwich. You can't taste it very well. There's still the saltiness of the ham, but it's not very strong, and you can't tell what kind of cheese it is.

21

'People say I eat too much'

Simon is a bit chubby and his friends call him names behind his back. This is Simon's story ...

'They tell me I eat too much, but I'm always hungry. Even when I'm not hungry, I still want to eat. I've always got a snack in my pocket. At school they call me names like fatso, and worse. Nobody knows how awful I feel when I can't do the rope climb or gymnastics. Some kids wait for me to fall down so they can laugh at me. I wish they wouldn't tease me.'

It's hard for Simon. He's too plump and children laugh at him. He's got into the bad habit of eating too many snacks. He especially likes pastries, chocolate bars, pizzas and fries. These are really rich, fatty foods which have more kilojoules than other foods. The extra energy from these foods is stored as fat in his body.

Obesity increases the risk of heart and artery problems, and makes people's lives miserable. But if people can change they will find that fresh vegetables are just as tasty as potato chips, and strawberries are as delicious as cake.

100 ml of skim milk contains: 10 g sugar, 7 g protein and 240 mg calcium

100 ml of soft drink contains: 25 g sugar, 0 g protein and 0 mg calcium!

It's just as dangerous to do the opposite of eating too much – if you don't eat enough, you don't get the energy you need. Your body and brain don't develop properly, you get sick more easily, feel tired, and may even become seriously ill.

Did you know?

When choosing between foods with the same amount of kilojoules, the ones with larger amounts of other nutrients are better for your body.

23

'I don't like red meat'

Josephine can't stand red meat. Maybe you're the same. (Or is it cauliflower you hate?)

This is Josephine's story ...

'I don't have a problem – it's really my mother. She really wants me to eat red meat. She always says, "Eat it, or there'll be trouble". But I just can't. I hate every kind of meat there is. Except maybe chicken. It's not because I'm worried about killing animals (although I do feel a bit sorry for the chickens). But I hate the smell of steak cooking. I don't think I'll ever change my mind.'

Did you know?

In dishes from countries where meat is scarce or expensive, the combination of cereals and pulses makes up for the lack of meat protein. For example, Moroccan couscous mixes wheat and chickpeas; and Indian recipes use rice and lentils together.

So Josephine doesn't like meat. Fair enough. She might change her mind as she grows up, or she might continue to avoid it. But it's important to understand that if you never eat certain foods, you may end up with a deficiency.

We don't need to eat meat every day, but it can provide us with very good protein, iron and other essential minerals.

Some people choose to be vegetarians. They replace meat with other foods; they combine cereals and pulses and eat dairy products to provide other proteins. Maybe Josephine will become a vegetarian.

'I'd like to live on pancakes with jam'

Melanie loves sweets, chocolate and pancakes. But can she really live on these alone?

This is Melanie's story ...

'My favourite food is pancakes with jam, or maybe with chocolate syrup. Why should I eat anything else if that's what I like? It's a battle with my parents. They want me to eat the food they cook, like all those stews. I think they look like catfood, and ham smells like the stuff I feed my goldfish.'

'I like strawberry tarts and chocolate éclairs as well. But my parents keep saying, "You can only have some if you finish your steak and beans". So meal times aren't a whole lot of fun …'

'It's strange, I often get hungry between meals. I have to be pretty organised and carry a few caramels in my pocket.'

You have to admit Melanie is not being very smart. Sugary foods are high in energy but low in nutrients. If you don't eat anything but sugar, your body starts storing fat and it feels hungrier and hungrier. And there's another problem with sugars: they'll make great big holes in your teeth.

Warning! Sugar is hiding in many foods: biscuits, cakes, soft drinks, ice cream, breakfast cereals … and even in tomato sauce! That's why it can be easy to eat too much sugar without realising it.

Cereals and pulses contain a kind of sugar called slow sugars (or complex carbohydrates). They don't taste sweet, and they are digested very slowly. This means they supply the body – especially the brain – with the energy it needs for several hours.

Before competing in sports, one of the best things for an athlete to eat is a big plate of spaghetti!

Where does food come from?

Some foods are harvested from nature and eaten just as they are. Other foods are made by hand or in factories. Some are made from plants; others from animals.

Cereals, fruit and vegetables come onto the market according to the season. Meat (beef, pork, chicken) is from farms; shellfish and fresh fish are gathered from the sea or raised in large ponds on fish farms.

Other foods are made from a combination of ingredients. Bread is made from wheat flour, water and yeast (which makes the dough rise). Cheeses are made in factories or on farms, from the milk of cows, sheep or goats. Sausages are made from pork or beef, spices and preservatives, all piped into a thin casing.

Did you know?

Pasta is made from wheat flour mixed with water. The dough is kneaded and placed in machines that create a range of different shapes: shells, bow ties or long noodles. Sometimes eggs are added to the recipe. The pasta is dried and packaged for sale.

Find out: How is tomato sauce made? Where do your bananas come from? What are free-range eggs?

Experiment

Make your own butter

You need some fresh cream. Leave it to reach room temperature. Put about six tablespoons of the cream into a bowl and beat well (or shake it in an airtight container). Soon you'll see yellow specks start to appear and a watery liquid (buttermilk) will separate out. Keep beating and the butter will begin to form. Tip it into a sieve to drain the liquid. Put the butter back in the bowl with a little water and mix until it forms a ball. Repeat by straining and beating until the butter looks right. You might like to add a little salt.

Experiment

Make your own yoghurt

1. Bring some water to boil in a large pot. Slowly warm a litre of milk in a saucepan to exactly 53°C – it must not boil. Use a food thermometer to check.

2. Stir one small pottle of plain unsweetened yoghurt into the warm milk and fill eight small containers with the mixture.

3. Take the large pot of water off the heat and place the small containers in it, making sure no water gets into the milk mixture. Put the lid on the pot and leave it undisturbed overnight. The next day, you will have eight fresh yoghurts.

[Ask a grown-up to help you with this experiment.]

The story of milk

What can be made from cow's milk? Here are some of the many ways this precious liquid is used.

Milk is almost a complete food for humans. It contains protein, fats, sugar (called lactose) and even vitamins. One of the greatest benefits of milk is that it contains lots of calcium. This mineral is essential for bones, and so it is needed by growing children. To build a really strong skeleton you should have dairy products every day: maybe a glass of milk, some yoghurt or a piece of cheese.

1. A cow doesn't make milk unless she has a calf. After the baby is born, the mother produces milk to feed it.

2. Twice a day, seven days a week, the cows have to be milked. Usually this is done with machines. The milk is sucked from the cow's teats, the way it would be by the calf.

3. Next, the milk is transported in refrigerated trucks to the milk factory. Here it's packaged into cartons or bottles, or turned into cream, cheese and yoghurt.

4. It goes through a pasteurising machine that kills any bugs, and then it is bottled and refrigerated. Another treatment called UHT (where the milk is heated to an Ultra High Temperature) allows the milk to be stored at room temperature.

5. To make cream, milk is poured into a separator machine. It rotates at high speed to separate the fat (the cream) from the milk.

6. Butter is made from cream by beating it vigorously.

7. To make cheese, the milk has to be curdled by adding cultures. The curds are then placed in moulds of different sizes and drained. The cheeses are then turned out of their moulds and stored in a maturing room. In France, there are over 400 kinds of cheese!

Did you know?

A dairy cow makes around 30 litres of milk each day. Therefore, it needs to eat between 60 and 80 kilograms of grass or hay, and drink 50 litres of water every day!

The history of food

The fruits and vegetables we buy didn't always grow in our local gardens. Many of the food plants that are well-known today have spent centuries journeying around the world. They were taken in ships or carried by traders' caravans to be adopted in countries far from their original home.

Most of the world's vegetables, fruits and cereals originally came from the Middle East or the Mediterranean. Wheat, barley, lentils and peas were grown for more than 9,500 years in those places. They slowly moved further north to areas where only a few food plants grew, such as cabbages and lettuces. It took a long time: for example, wheat took over a thousand years to reach Europe. In each new place, the plants had to adapt to new climates.

Many other plants were imported after the discovery of the Americas by the Spanish conquistadors. The tomatoes we eat today are descended from a small wild variety of cherry tomatoes that grew in Central America. The Aztecs called them 'tomatl'.

It was 200 years before anyone in Europe showed an interest in tomatoes. First to do so was Italy, where tomato sauce was made in the 18th century.

The onion and the eggplant both came from India. Peppers and zucchini came from Mexico. Apricots and peaches originated in Central Asia. Strawberries came from two places, North America and Chile.

Did you know?

Potatoes come from the Andes, in South America. They were taken to Europe by Pizarro, a conquistador, in 1560. In many countries with cooler climates, people ate potatoes as the main part of their diet because they are easy to grow and very healthy. In France this root vegetable was hated for a long time. It was called 'pig bread' because it was only used to feed pigs.

Eating through the ages

The first humans didn't eat fries, and the rich ladies of the Middle Ages didn't feast on chocolate ... So what *did* our ancestors eat?

The first humans spent a lot of time looking for things to eat. Farming hadn't been invented, so wild cereals and fruits were their main foods. Hunting provided them with meat, which was eaten raw until fire was discovered about 500,000 years ago. Learning how to cook food meant that people began to prepare and eat their meals together – the ancient origins of the kitchen and dining room.

Farming began about 10,000 years ago. People started to grow small crops and raise cattle, sheep and pigs. This was a new way of providing food, mostly from cereals (wheat, rye, barley). Cheese-making was discovered by accident: a calf's stomach was used to store milk, and the rennet in it made the milk curdle and dry – creating the first cheese.

The daily diet of the Romans included vegetables, porridge and flatbreads. They had regular feasts, where guests spent hours eating. They lay on couches, drank honeyed wine and ate carefully-prepared meat dishes, oysters and dried fruit.

There was a great variety of food in the Middle Ages. Soups were made with cooked wheat, rye and barley. People liked strong-tasting dishes (using spices), acidic flavours (vinegar) and sweet ones (honey, dates, raisins), as well as game, pies, and cheeses that could be stored.

Did you know?

Over the last few decades, people in developed countries have been eating less fresh fruit and pulses. At the same time, there has been a trend towards eating foods that have high sugar and fat content – like sugary drinks, hamburgers, fries, creamy desserts, cakes and pastries. These foods may be high in energy but they don't contain many nutrients. They often have no protein, complex carbohydrates, vitamins or minerals.

Chocolate, tea, sugar and coffee were taken to Europe by sailors in the 16th century, but only the wealthy nobility consumed them. It was only in the 17th and 18th centuries that these foods from the Caribbean would be on nearly everyone's table.

The first restaurants were not opened until the 19th century. At the same time there was a lot of progress in preserving foods, mostly thanks to pasteurisation.

In the 20th century eating habits changed again. Preserved food was to be found in cans on shop shelves, frozen food was invented, and prepared dishes were made in factories.

Maybe one day we will be fed by swallowing pills! Would you like that?

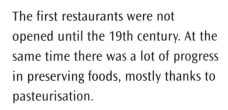

Eating in other countries

Food varies from country to country. What fascinating eating habits people have — everything from seaweed to insects and snails.

Cereals are still the basic diet of all the peoples on Earth.

Wheat is the most widely-grown cereal in the world. It can be prepared in many ways: cracked wheat, bulghur wheat, couscous, semolina, flour for bread, cake, and pasta.

Rice is the main food in many countries. In India it's flavoured with a delicious spice called cardamom; in South America it's served with a red bean stew; and in Spain it's flavoured with saffron, as the base of *paella*.

Humans are omnivores. This means we can eat everything, plants and animals.

Foods that are unknown in one country can be special treats in another. In certain countries, some people even eat monkey, snake or turtle.

In Japan, people eat seaweed, which is very healthy, and raw fish with a sweet and sour flavouring.

In China, it's quite normal for people to eat ducks' feet by sucking out the middle. They also eat birds' nests and shark fins, which are expensive delicacies.

Would you like to be served grubs for lunch? You may pull a face, but in some African and Asian countries people often eat insects like grilled grasshoppers, or red ants to spice up the soup. These tiny creatures were also eaten by our prehistoric ancestors and are a useful source of protein.

Do you think that's gross? How about going to France to eat frogs' legs, raw oysters, and snails in garlic sauce?

Experiment

Tell a friend about some new food you have discovered recently and enjoyed. And try to taste an unusual food that you've always thought was horrible.

Cracked eggs and mad cows

We hear a lot of nasty things about food: poisoned chicken and 'mad cow' disease. Should we put everything we eat under the microscope to check it first?

It's true that some toxic bacteria have been found in chicken meat and cracked eggs, and you might have heard about cows going mad, or water being polluted with sewerage.

But in industrialised countries, food is carefully inspected, from the farmer's field or milking shed to the food you find on supermarket shelves. For example, the temperature of frozen foods is monitored to make sure it doesn't cause any micro-organisms to grow that might poison people.

That's also the reason for the 'use by' dates on the packaging of many products.

But there are still accidents sometimes. Sometimes dangerous chemicals get into food, especially in big cities. Pollution is created by factories and cars, and it moves easily through the air and waterways. Poisons may get onto plants and be eaten by chickens or by cows grazing on grass.

Finally the chemicals reach people through meat or milk. Over many years, these poisons can build up in the human body, and it takes a long time to get rid of them.

How could chemicals get into our drinking water? Chemicals called nitrates come from fertilisers which are spread on fields to increase crops. These nitrates travel through the soil or are washed into underground wells and into the water supply. Nitrates can be dangerous to humans' health, especially for bottle-fed babies.

Did you know?

GMOs (Genetically Modified Organisms) are plant species that have been altered by scientists in a laboratory. For example, some have been made resistant to certain chemical weedkillers. The GMO plant will grow, while the weeds around it will die.

Unfortunately there are some problems with GMOs. There's the risk that the features of these GMO plants could cross over to nearby plants, and weeds may become resistant to weedkillers. Also, the old plant varieties might be lost forever. Since the GMOs are resistant to weedkillers, farmers might have to use even more chemicals.

GMO plants soak in large amounts of chemicals from the weedkillers. When we eat these plants, it's possible we might absorb large amounts of chemicals too. That's why many people are concerned about this new science.

There are other health risks with food. Shellfish and deli meats can sometimes be contaminated by very dangerous bacteria called salmonella.

So-called 'mad' cows passed the terrible Creutzfeldt-Jakob disease to humans. These quiet grazers are herbivores. But to make them grow faster, some farmers gave them food made from the offal, bones and fat of other animals. The cows picked up a disease from these scraps, and people who ate the meat of the cow picked it up too.

But don't be put off eating! The risks of food contamination were much more wide-spread in the past.

Food groups

Milk and dairy products

(cheese, yoghurt, butter)
These provide calcium, protein, fat, and vitamins A and B.

Meat, fish and eggs

These supply protein, fat, and vitamins A and B.

Fruits and vegetables

These supply sugar (carbohydrates), fibre, vitamin C and minerals.

Potatoes, legumes and cereals

(lentils, beans, bread, pasta, rice, corn)
These provide 'slow' sugars (complex carbohydrates), protein and vitamin B.

Fats

(oil, butter, cream)
These supply fats and vitamin A (in butter and cream).

Liquids

(water, flavoured drinks)
These provide water, mineral salts and sometimes sugar.

Sweets and cakes

These supply 'fast' sugars.

How much sugar?

It all depends on how much you eat.

The same amount of slow sugar is found in all these foods: 100 g of bread, 370 g of potatoes, 250 g of pasta, 180 g of rice, 75 g of oatmeal.

The same amount of fast sugar is found in all these foods: 4 teaspoons of sugar, 4 sweets, 1 dessertspoon of honey, 1 glass of lemonade, 6 squares of chocolate.

Recommended quantities

Calcium

For children aged eight to 12, a daily intake of 900 mg of calcium is recommended.

There are 300 mg of calcium in: 2 yoghurts; 40 g of cheese; 500 mls of milk; 1 kg of oranges; 850 g of cabbage.

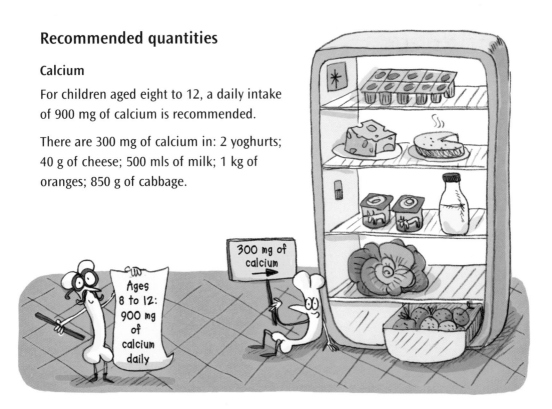

Protein

Around 60 g of protein is the recommended daily intake for a ten year old.

There are 18 to 20 g of protein in: ½ litre of milk; two eggs; 100 g of steak; 70 g of cheese; 4 yoghurts; 100 g of fish

Balanced meals

It's not hard to eat sensibly and well. There's no need to do any exact computing of kilojoules — just use your common sense!

To eat well, eat a variety of foods. You need to eat from every food group regularly. From some food groups you need to eat something every day. Only sweet foods are not essential.

Did you know?

Breakfast is a very important meal. Always eat before you leave for school, otherwise you'll feel very tired by mid-morning. It's been suggested that breakfast should be about a quarter of your food intake for the day. Not hungry when you first get up? Wait a little while: have a shower, drink a glass of water, set the table. Try a variety of breakfast foods: maybe a fruit yoghurt, a boiled egg, cereal, some grated apple with oats …

This pyramid suggests a healthy amount that can be eaten from different food groups. As you go down the pyramid you can eat more of each group.

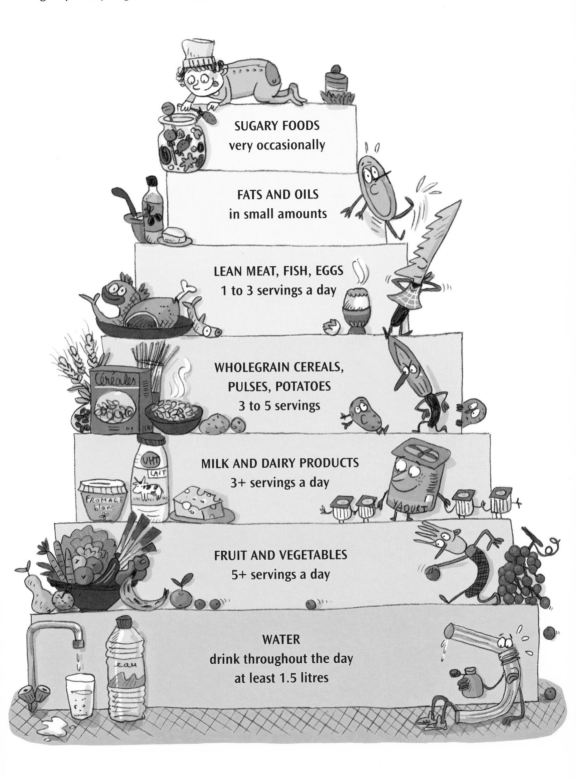

SUGARY FOODS
very occasionally

FATS AND OILS
in small amounts

LEAN MEAT, FISH, EGGS
1 to 3 servings a day

WHOLEGRAIN CEREALS,
PULSES, POTATOES
3 to 5 servings

MILK AND DAIRY PRODUCTS
3+ servings a day

FRUIT AND VEGETABLES
5+ servings a day

WATER
drink throughout the day
at least 1.5 litres

In a nutshell

Whether you like every food or not many, here are some suggestions.

Even if you don't like cauliflower, try this harmless trick: try a mouthful every time it's on your plate. It won't always have been cooked by the same person, and it won't always look or taste the same. You might be surprised one day – tastes do change. Maybe you'll come to like it.

Try to eat in a quiet atmosphere, with no fuss or noise. Just take your time – it will help your digestion.

Avoid sweet or salty snacks between meals. And avoid highly processed foods: wholegrain bread is more nutritious than white bread.

Maybe you have a problem with food: you eat too much and you don't know how to stop. Talk to your parents about it or ask them to take you to see a dietitian.

Eat as wide a range of foods as you can. Variety is the key to good health.

Eat moderate amounts depending on how active you are: if you ski for three hours you can eat more high-energy food than if you just sit in front of the TV.

Now it's your turn: try to plan a delicious and balanced diet.

Recipes to tempt your tastebuds

Party tomatoes

1. Take four large tomatoes and cut off their tops. Scoop out most of the flesh and juice.

2. In a bowl, mix 100 g of cooked shrimp (or canned tuna), an avocado cut into cubes, the tomato pulp, 4 tablespoons of sweetcorn kernels, and some grapefruit cut into small pieces (optional).

3. Fill the tomato shells with this tasty mixture and place them on a platter. You may like to decorate it with hard-boiled eggs.

4. Make a dressing with the juice of a lemon, a teaspoon of mustard, a tablespoon of sour cream and a dash of olive oil.

Potato pancakes

1. Grate a large potato into a bowl.

2. Add 50 g of grated cheese, a pinch of nutmeg, a beaten egg, a tablespoon of flour, and a little salt and pepper.

4. Heat a small amount of oil in a non-stick frypan and cook the pancake on both sides until golden brown. Serve with a fresh green salad to make a great meal.

3. Stir all the ingredients together.

Rice hedgehogs

1. Leave 200 g of white rice to soak in cold water for two hours. Drain it and spread it out on a paper towel. Wash five button mushrooms and chop into small pieces.

2. In a bowl, mix 200 g of minced beef, the mushrooms, two chopped onions, a beaten egg and a crushed clove of garlic. Mix well with a fork.

3. Make sure your hands are clean. Shape small amounts of the mixture into balls (about twenty) and roll them in the rice until they are coated with it. Place the hedgehogs in a steamer, and put it in a pot filled with water. Cook for at least 30 minutes.

4. Add little raisins for the eyes and nose and serve with tomato sauce or with soy sauce.

Tropical chicken kebabs

1. Make a marinade for the chicken pieces the day before. In a bowl, mix together the juice of a lemon, a tablespoon of honey, some salt and pepper, a crushed clove of garlic, some grated ginger, a teaspoon of curry powder, and half a teaspoon each of cumin and coriander. Add a small amount of chilli powder if you dare!

2. Cut four chicken breasts into cubes and pour over the marinade. Cover and leave them to soak in the refrigerator overnight. Stir occasionally.

3. An hour before dinner time, prepare the kebabs: drain the chicken cubes and thread them onto the skewers.

4. Put the skewers into an oven dish and cook them in a moderate oven, basting them occasionally with the leftover marinade. When they are golden brown and cooked through, serve on a bed of rice.

The food quiz

1. Cheese is usually made from:

a) Sour cream and donkey's milk
b) Soy milk
c) Cow's milk

2. Say whether the following foods are animal or plant products:

- milk
- flour
- cherries
- sugar
- eggs
- butter
- bread
- walnuts
- blackcurrant juice
- minced beef

3. You need to drink some water every day

☐ True ☐ False

4. It's not necessary for people to eat meat.

☐ True ☐ False

5. Popeye was right: spinach really is a source of iron.

☐ True ☐ False

6. A packet of chips, a chocolate bar and a soft drink is a healthy replacement for a meal.

☐ True ☐ False

7. Potatoes and bread make you fat.

☐ True ☐ False

8. If you skip breakfast, you'll feel very tired later.

☐ True ☐ False

Answers

1. c) Most cheese is made from cow's milk — although goat's and sheep's milk may also be used.

2. Milk, eggs, butter and minced beef are animal products. Cherries, flour, sugar, bread, blackcurrant juice and walnuts are plant products.

3. True. You should drink at least one and a half litres of water every day. It's best to drink pure water rather than sugary drinks. They are less thirst-quenching than water and contain sugar your body doesn't need.

4. True. Meat does contain a lot of essential elements (protein and high levels of iron) but it can be replaced by other foods, like eggs and tofu.

5. True. There is iron in spinach, but there's much more in chicken liver, red meat, sardines, eggs and lentils.

6. False. These foods have high fat content and quickly supply a lot of energy, but they have very little nutritional value (no vitamins or complex carbohydrates). Once their energy has been used up, they'll leave you hungry and wanting to snack.

7. False. Potatoes are carbohydrates, and bread is made from cereals. These foods (and rice and pasta) contain essential carbohydrates which are the most important energy source. It is dangerous to drop them from your diet. What can make us fat is what we put on them: lots of sour cream, butter, jam....

8. True. Breakfast is your first meal in at least ten hours, so it is important to eat properly to start the day or you'll feel tired by 11am. The ideal breakfast would be a piece of fruit or a glass of pure fruit juice, a bowl of cereal with milk or yoghurt, toast (with butter, vegemite or honey) and even a boiled egg!

Mini dictionary

Culture: Micro-organisms that cause fermentation.

Dietitian: Specialist in nutrition.

Deficiency: Lack of a nutrient that is essential for good health; may lead to disease.

Food chain: Series of relationships between living creatures, linked together by the foods they eat.

Herbivores: Animals that eat only plants.

Kilojoule (kJ): Unit of measurement of the energy supplied by foods.

Nutrients: Simple food elements that are absorbed directly by the body. Proteins, sugars (or carbohydrates), fats, vitamins, minerals.

Obesity: Being overweight.

Oesophagus: Canal linking the mouth to the stomach.

Omnivore: Person or animal that eats both plants and animals.

Pasteurisation: A technique invented by Louis Pasteur to kill the microbes that occur in food when it is not to be eaten immediately.

Pulses: Plants that make foods such as peas, beans and lentils.

Taste buds: Tiny organs on the tongue that allow us to sense flavours.

Vegetarians: People who do not eat meat.

Some useful websites

www.foodafactoflife.org.uk

www.freshforkids.com.au